Math in Focus®

Singapore Math®
by Marshall Cavendish

Extra Practice and Homework

Program Consultant
Dr. Fong Ho Kheong

Author
Dr. Ng Wee Leng

Marshall Cavendish
Education

U.S. Distributor

Houghton Mifflin Harcourt.
The Learning Company™

Course 1A

© 2020 Marshall Cavendish Education Pte Ltd

Published by Marshall Cavendish Education
Times Centre, 1 New Industrial Road, Singapore 536196
Customer Service Hotline: (65) 6213 9688
US Office Tel: (1-914) 332 8888 | Fax: (1-914) 332 8882
E-mail: cs@mceducation.com
Website: www.mceducation.com

Distributed by
Houghton Mifflin Harcourt
125 High Street
Boston, MA 02110
Tel: 617-351-5000
Website: www.hmhco.com/programs/math-in-focus

First published 2020

All rights reserved. No part of this publication may be reproduced, stored in a retrieval system or transmitted, in any form or by any means, electronic, mechanical, photocopying, recording or otherwise, without the prior written permission of Marshall Cavendish Education. If you have received these materials as examination copies free of charge, Marshall Cavendish Education retains the rights to the materials and they may not be resold. Resale of examination copies is strictly prohibited.

Marshall Cavendish and *Math in Focus*® are registered trademarks of Times Publishing Limited.

Singapore Math® is a trademark of Singapore Math Inc.® and Marshall Cavendish Education Pte Ltd.

ISBN 978-0-358-10308-0

Printed in Singapore

3 4 5 6 7 8 9 10   1401   26 25 24 23 22
4500840211   B C D E F

The cover image shows a barn owl.
Owls live in trees or sometimes in the top of barns. They are mostly nocturnal, so they usually come out at night. They have large eyes that are fixed in place, so they rely on their ability to turn their necks 270° to scan their surroundings. Their ears are asymmetrically shaped and positioned, allowing their brains to calculate the exact location of their prey in total darkness. They are excellent hunters who eat mostly rodents.

Contents

© 2020 Marshall Cavendish Education Pte Ltd

Chapter 6   **Percent**

© 2020 Marshall Cavendish Education Pte Ltd

Preface

Welcome!

Math in F☉cus® *Extra Practice and Homework* is written to complement the Student Edition in your learning journey.

The book provides carefully constructed activities and problems that parallel what you have learned in the Student Edition.

- **Activities** are designed to help you achieve proficiency in the math concepts and to develop confidence in your mathematical abilities.

- **MATH JOURNAL** is included to provide you with opportunities to reflect on the learning in the chapter.

- **PUT ON YOUR THINKING CAP!** allows you to improve your critical thinking and problem-solving skills, as well as to be challenged as you solve problems in novel ways.

You may use a calculator whenever ▤ appears.

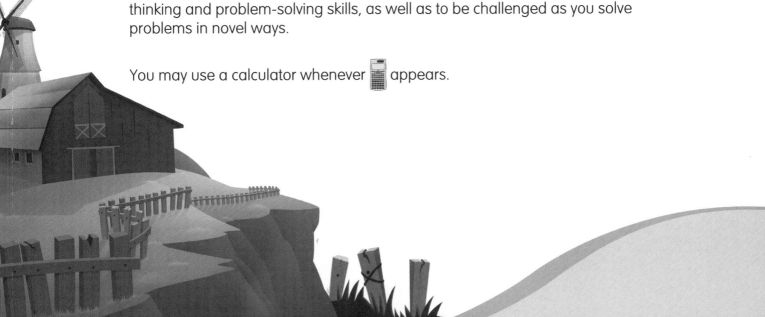

BLANK

Name: _____ Date: _____

Extra Practice and Homework
Whole Numbers, Prime Numbers, and Prime Factorization

Activity 2   Common Factors and Multiples

Find the common factors of each pair of numbers.

1 18 and 50

2 25 and 75

3 36 and 90

4 56 and 80

Find the greatest common factor of each pair of numbers.

5 18 and 27

6 42 and 54

7 49 and 70

8 40 and 85

Find the first three common multiples of each pair of numbers.

9 2 and 5

10 5 and 6

11 9 and 21

12 12 and 18

© 2020 Marshall Cavendish Education Pte Ltd

Find the least common multiple of each pair of numbers.

13 8 and 12

14 12 and 20

15 18 and 30

16 18 and 54

Find the greatest common factor of each set of numbers.

17 12, 48, and 60

18 40, 66, and 78

Find the least common multiple of each set of numbers.

19 5, 20, and 30

20 24, 36, and 54

© 2020 Marshall Cavendish Education Pte Ltd

Find the greatest common factor and the least common multiple of each set of numbers.

21 14, 28, and 49

22 40, 64, and 72

Solve.

23 Kevin has a plain ribbon and a striped ribbon. The length of the plain ribbon is 54 inches and the length of the striped ribbon is 90 inches. He wants to cut the ribbons into pieces of the same length.

    a Find the greatest possible length that he can cut for each piece, so that no ribbon will be left unused.

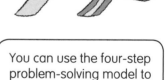

You can use the four-step problem-solving model to help you.

    b Write the sum of the two lengths and factor out the number you found in **a**.

© 2020 Marshall Cavendish Education Pte Ltd

2 Common Factors and Multiples   **5**

24 A box of cards can be shared equally among 4, 5, or 6 students, with 3 cards left over each time. What is the least possible number of cards in the box?

25 Bus services A, B, and C leave Boston Interchange every 3, 6, and 21 minutes respectively. All three bus services first leave the interchange at 6 A.M. What time will the three bus services next leave the interchange at the same time?

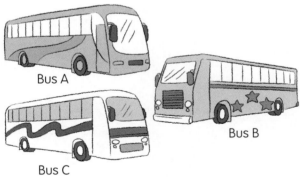

Bus A

Bus B

Bus C

© 2020 Marshall Cavendish Education Pte Ltd

Chapter 1

Extra Practice and Homework
Whole Numbers, Prime Numbers, and Prime Factorization

Activity 3 Squares and Cubes

Find the square of each number.

1 4

2 5

3 8

4 14

Find the cube of each number.

5 2

6 7

7 12

8 15

Solve.

9 List the perfect squares between 50 and 300 that are even numbers.

> A perfect square is even when the number being squared is also even.

10 List the perfect cubes between 100 and 350 that are odd numbers.

© 2020 Marshall Cavendish Education Pte Ltd

Find the value of each expression.

11 $6^2 + 4^3$

12 $8^3 - 5^2$

13 $3^2 \times 2^3$

14 $9^3 \div 4^3$

15 $3^2 + 7^3 + 4^3$

16 $10^3 + 8^2 - 5^3$

17 $5^3 \times 2^2 - 4^3$

18 $8^2 \div 2^3 + 7^3$

© 2020 Marshall Cavendish Education Pte Ltd

19 $6^2 \times 2^3 + 4^2$

20 $9^3 \div 3^2 - 5^2$

Solve.

21   Given that $15^2 = 225$, find the square of 150.

What is the relationship between 15 and 150?

22   Given that $9^3 = 729$, find the cube of 90.

23   Evaluate $15^2 - 12^2 + 10^3$.

24   Find two consecutive numbers whose cubes have a difference of 127.

You can use guess and check to solve the problem.

© 2020 Marshall Cavendish Education Pte Ltd

25 Eric needed square pieces of paper, each with sides of length 6 centimeters, to fold origami. First, he cut a square piece of paper with sides of length 84 centimeters, into the square pieces he needed. Then, he cut another piece of square paper with sides of length 72 centimeters to get more square pieces, of the required size.

    a Find the number of square pieces he had after cutting the square paper with sides of length 84 centimeters. Write your answer as a square number.

    b Find the number of square pieces he had after cutting the square paper with sides of length 72 centimeters. Write your answer as a square number.

    c How many square pieces did Eric get in all?

26 Similar ice cubes were packed closely to one another inside a big cubic container with edge length of 75 centimeters, without gaps between the cubes. Some of the ice cubes were later transferred into a small cubic container with edge length of 25 centimeters. The edge length of each ice cube was 5 centimeters. How many ice cubes were left in the big cubic container?

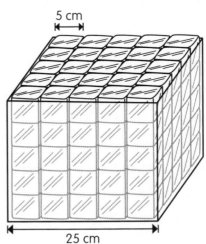

5 cm

25 cm

© 2020 Marshall Cavendish Education Pte Ltd

Mathematical Habit 8 Look for patterns

The following shows three square numbers.

36	225	400

a Write each square number as a product of its prime factors.

b How many times does each of the prime factors repeat for each square number?

c Are the number of times in b odd or even? Explain how to tell whether a number is a square number by looking at the product of its prime factors.

© 2020 Marshall Cavendish Education Pte Ltd

1 [Mathematical Habit **8**] **Look for patterns**

a Write 756 as a product of its prime factors.

b Write 3,528 as a product of its prime factors.

c Without using a calculator, find 3,528 ÷ 756.

Look for the common factors of 756 and 3,528.

2 [Mathematical Habit **1**] **Persevere in solving problems**

A rectangular game board measuring 136 inches by 96 inches is divided into squares of equal sizes.

a Find the greatest possible length of the side of a square.

b Find the least number of squares the game board is divided into.

© 2020 Marshall Cavendish Education Pte Ltd

Extra Practice and Homework
Number Lines and Negative Numbers

Chapter 2

Activity 1   The Number Line

Complete each number line by filling in the missing values.

1

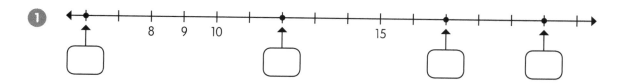

8   9   10   15

2

40   41   42

3

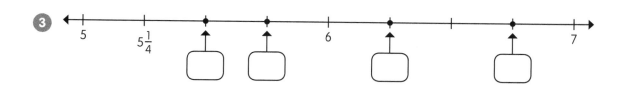

5        $5\frac{1}{4}$ 6   7

4

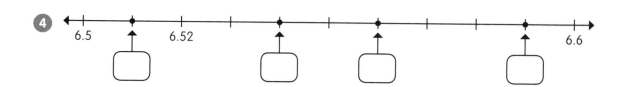

6.5   6.52   6.6

© 2020 Marshall Cavendish Education Pte Ltd

Draw a horizontal number line to represent each set of numbers.

5 Even numbers between 10 and 25

6 Whole numbers greater than 25 but less than 36

7 Mixed numbers between 2 and 4, with an interval of $\frac{1}{5}$ between each pair of mixed numbers

8 Decimals from 8.4 to 9.5, with an interval of 0.1 between each pair of decimals

© 2020 Marshall Cavendish Education Pte Ltd

Draw a vertical number line to represent each set of numbers.

9 Whole numbers greater than 35 but less than 42

10 Mixed numbers between 7 and 9, with an interval of $\frac{1}{4}$ between each pair of mixed numbers

© 2020 Marshall Cavendish Education Pte Ltd

Compare each pair of numbers using > or <. Draw a number line to help you.

11. $\frac{7}{4} \bigcirc 2\frac{1}{4}$

12. $8\frac{2}{5} \bigcirc 8\frac{2}{7}$

13. $6\frac{3}{5} \bigcirc 6\frac{5}{6}$

14. $12.1 \bigcirc 11.2$

15. $84.97 \bigcirc 84.79$

16. $67.03 \bigcirc 76.30$

Draw a horizontal line from 6 to 8 to represent each set of numbers.

17. $6\frac{1}{3}$, $6\frac{5}{6}$, $6\frac{1}{6}$, $7\frac{2}{3}$, $7\frac{1}{3}$, and $7\frac{5}{6}$

Draw a horizontal line between 1 and 3 to represent each set of numbers.

18. 1.5, 2.5, 2.25, 1.25, and 2.75

© 2020 Marshall Cavendish Education Pte Ltd

Compare each pair of numbers using > or <. Draw a number line to help you.

19 $\frac{1}{2}$ ◯ 0.3

20 2.5 ◯ $2\frac{3}{4}$

You can rewrite each fraction as a decimal to compare.

21 4.25 ◯ $4\frac{2}{5}$

22 $\frac{7}{5}$ ◯ 1.75

23 8.7 ◯ $8\frac{2}{7}$

24 $12\frac{5}{8}$ ◯ 12.58

Solve.

25 The perimeter of a square photo album is $12\frac{1}{3}$ inches. The perimeter of a rectangular photo album is $12\frac{3}{8}$ inches. Write an inequality comparing the two perimeters.

 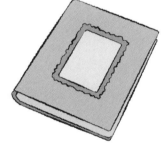

Perimeter = $12\frac{1}{3}$ in.   Perimeter = $12\frac{3}{8}$ in.

© 2020 Marshall Cavendish Education Pte Ltd

26 A white rope is 2.4 yards long. A gray rope is $2\frac{3}{4}$ yards long. Which rope is longer? How much longer?

2.4 yards $2\frac{3}{4}$ yards

27 A jug contains 1.45 liters of apple juice. A bottle contains $1\frac{11}{25}$ liters of apple juice. Which container holds less apple juice? How much less?

1.45 liters $1\frac{11}{25}$ liters

© 2020 Marshall Cavendish Education Pte Ltd

Extra Practice and Homework
Number Lines and Negative Numbers

Activity 2   Negative Numbers

Write a positive or negative number to represent each situation.

1 A profit of $280

2 A loss of 123 yards

3 2,300 feet below sea level

4 A credit of $6,700

5 7°F above zero

6 7°C below zero

Complete each number line by filling in the missing values.

7

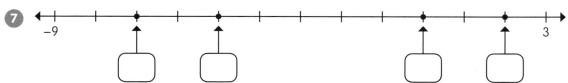

8

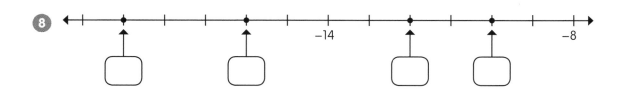

© 2020 Marshall Cavendish Education Pte Ltd

Write the opposite of each number.

9 4

10 −15

11 −200

12 3,200

Draw a horizontal number line to represent each set of numbers.

13 Even negative numbers from −9 to −1

14 Odd numbers from −8 to 2

© 2020 Marshall Cavendish Education Pte Ltd

Draw a vertical number line to represent each set of numbers.

15 Odd numbers between −5 and 1

16 Numbers from −4 to 2

Use the number line to compare each pair of numbers using > or <.

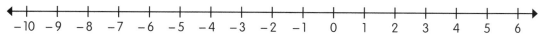

17 −8 ◯ −4

18 −3 ◯ −5

19 −4 ◯ 5

20 2 ◯ −6

21 −1 ◯ 1

22 −9 ◯ 3

© 2020 Marshall Cavendish Education Pte Ltd

Complete each inequality using > or <.

23 −8 ◯ 0

24 3 ◯ −3

25 8 ◯ −12

26 −14 ◯ −15

27 −29 ◯ −22

28 −42 ◯ 35

Order the numbers in each set from least to greatest.

29 −15, 20, 0, −120, 43, and −300

30 18, 210, −20, −309, 502, and −40

Order the numbers in each set from greatest to least.

31 −10, −65, 110, 80, −280, and 505

32 52, −456, 75, −214, 18, and −123

Extra Practice and Homework Course 1A

© 2020 Marshall Cavendish Education Pte Ltd

Answer each question.

33 Name two numbers that are each 3 units away from −1. Give the opposites of these two numbers.

Draw a number line to help you.

34 Write an inequality using > or < for the following statement:

2,800 feet above sea level is higher than 1,500 feet below sea level.

© 2020 Marshall Cavendish Education Pte Ltd

35 Jack and Lily both started with 0 points at the beginning of a board game. During the game, Jack lost 220 points and Lily lost 180 points. Who had fewer points at the end? Write an inequality statement to compare their results at the end of the game.

Write a statement to describe each inequality.

36 $-127°C < -98°C$

37 $-\$48 > -\$84$

© 2020 Marshall Cavendish Education Pte Ltd

Extra Practice and Homework
Number Lines and Negative Numbers

Activity 3 Absolute Value

Use the number line to find the absolute value of each of the following numbers.

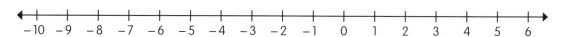

1 $|-9|$

2 $|-6|$

3 $|2|$

4 $|5|$

Write the absolute value of each number.

5 $|18|$

6 $|-216|$

7 $|672|$

8 $|-431|$

© 2020 Marshall Cavendish Education Pte Ltd

Complete each inequality using > or <.

9 $|-28|$ ◯ $|-44|$

10 $|-60|$ ◯ $|-50|$

11 $|200|$ ◯ $|-400|$

12 $|-190|$ ◯ $|208|$

13 $|-670|$ ◯ $|-580|$

14 $|890|$ ◯ $|-1,000|$

Answer each question.

15 Two numbers have an absolute value of 9. Which of the two numbers is greater than -5 ?

© 2020 Marshall Cavendish Education Pte Ltd

16 Two numbers have an absolute value of 4. Which of the two numbers is farther from 1 on the number line?

17 The amounts of money Mr. Brown, Ms. Clark, and Ms. Turner have in their bank accounts are recorded in the table below.

Name	Amount of Money in Bank Account
Mr. Brown	−$180
Ms. Carter	$90
Ms. Turner	−$290

a Who has the greatest amount of money in the bank account?

b Who has the least amount of money in the bank account?

© 2020 Marshall Cavendish Education Pte Ltd

18 The following table shows the highest and lowest daily temperatures of a park over a five-day period.

Day	Mon	Tue	Wed	Thu	Fri
Highest temperature (°C)	−6	3	−2	1	7
Lowest temperature (°C)	−11	−6	−7	−7	−8

a Which day has the greatest highest temperature?

b Which day has the smallest lowest temperature?

c Which days have temperatures below 0°C throughout the whole day?

d Arrange the highest temperatures in descending order.

© 2020 Marshall Cavendish Education Pte Ltd

Mathematical Habit 2 Use mathematical reasoning

The diagram shows a room thermometer and a clinical thermometer. The temperature readings are measured in degrees Celsius.

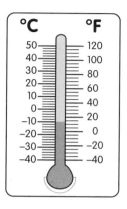
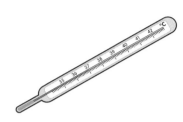

a Richard said that the scale of each thermometer is similar to a vertical or a horizontal number line. Do you agree? Explain.

b What are the temperature readings shown on both thermometers in degrees Celsius? Write an inequality using > or < to describe the temperatures. Explain what the temperatures could represent.

© 2020 Marshall Cavendish Education Pte Ltd

Mathematical Habit **1** Persevere in solving problems

An airplane is flying at 165 meters above sea level. A flock of birds is flying 90 meters above sea level. A submarine is 235 meters below sea level. A group of divers are diving along a reef at 82 meters below sea level.

a Which are below the sea level?

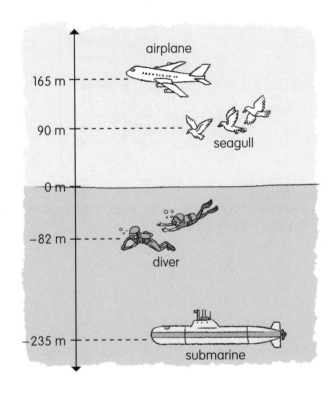

b Which are above the sea level?

c Which are farthest apart from each other?

d Which is closest to the sea level?

Extra Practice and Homework Course 1A

© 2020 Marshall Cavendish Education Pte Ltd

Chapter 3

Extra Practice and Homework
Fractions and Decimals

Activity 1 Dividing Fractions

Divide. Write each quotient in simplest form. Use bar models to help you.

1 $2 \div \frac{2}{3} =$ _____

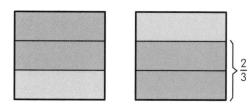

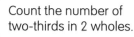

Count the number of two-thirds in 2 wholes.

2 $\frac{1}{2} \div \frac{1}{4} =$ _____

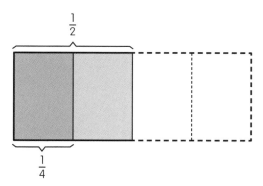

3 $\frac{3}{5} \div \frac{3}{10} =$ _____

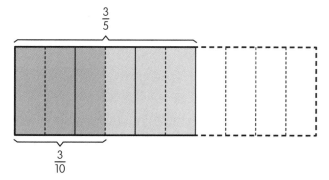

© 2020 Marshall Cavendish Education Pte Ltd

Draw a bar model to find each quotient.

4 $3 \div \frac{1}{6} =$ _____

5 $1 \div \frac{4}{5} =$ _____

6 $\frac{2}{5} \div \frac{1}{10} =$ _____

7 $\frac{2}{3} \div \frac{5}{9} =$ _____

© 2020 Marshall Cavendish Education Pte Ltd

Divide. Write each quotient in simplest form.

8 $3 \div \dfrac{2}{3} =$ _____

9 $7 \div \dfrac{5}{9} =$ _____

10 $10 \div \dfrac{4}{5} =$ _____

11 $\dfrac{2}{5} \div \dfrac{4}{9} =$ _____

12 $\dfrac{3}{7} \div \dfrac{1}{3} =$ _____

13 $\dfrac{1}{4} \div \dfrac{5}{12} =$ _____

14 $5\dfrac{1}{2} \div \dfrac{3}{5} =$ _____

15 $1\dfrac{2}{3} \div \dfrac{3}{4} =$ _____

© 2020 Marshall Cavendish Education Pte Ltd

Divide. Write each quotient in simplest form.

16 $\dfrac{1}{7} \div \dfrac{3}{2} =$ _____

17 $\dfrac{1}{4} \div \dfrac{9}{5} =$ _____

18 $\dfrac{1}{2} \div \dfrac{4}{3} =$ _____

19 $\dfrac{2}{3} \div \dfrac{9}{2} =$ _____

20 $\dfrac{4}{5} \div \dfrac{4}{3} =$ _____

21 $1\dfrac{3}{4} \div 8\dfrac{1}{6} =$ _____

22 $2\dfrac{1}{8} \div 4\dfrac{3}{4} =$ _____

23 $2\dfrac{3}{5} \div 4\dfrac{1}{3} =$ _____

© 2020 Marshall Cavendish Education Pte Ltd

Chapter 3

Extra Practice and Homework
Fractions and Decimals

Activity 2 Real-World Problems: Fractions

Solve.

1 Jacob had 3 kilograms of flour. He used $\frac{3}{4}$ kilogram of the flour to make bread every day. How many days did he take to finish all the flour?

How do you check your answer?

2 Jenna has $4\frac{1}{2}$ yards of thread. She cuts the thread into equal pieces such that each piece measures $\frac{1}{4}$ yard. How many pieces of thread does Jenna have?

© 2020 Marshall Cavendish Education Pte Ltd

3 Andrew drinks $\frac{2}{5}$ liter of orange juice each day. How many days does it take him to finish 3 liters of orange juice?

4 Arianna has 4 sheets of wrapping paper. Each sheet of wrapping paper has an area of 4 square feet. Arianna cuts the sheets of wrapping paper into pieces that measure $\frac{1}{2}$ square foot each. How many cut pieces are there altogether?

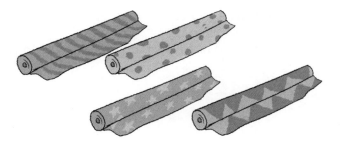

© 2020 Marshall Cavendish Education Pte Ltd

5 Ms. Morgan went for a vacation for 20 days. She spent $\frac{2}{5}$ of her vacation time in Asia and the rest in Europe. In Asia, she spent $\frac{1}{2}$ of her time in Thailand.

  a What fraction of her vacation time did Ms. Morgan spend in Thailand?

  b How many days did she spend in Thailand?

6 The area of a rectangular piece of cloth is $\frac{3}{4}$ square foot. The width of the cloth is $\frac{1}{2}$ foot. Find the length of the cloth.

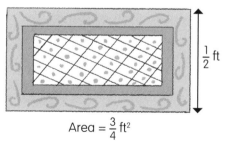

$\frac{1}{2}$ ft

Area $= \frac{3}{4}$ ft^2

© 2020 Marshall Cavendish Education Pte Ltd

7 The mass of a bag of walnuts was $5\frac{1}{4}$ kilograms. Mr. Nelson repacked the walnuts into smaller bags of equal mass. The mass of each bag was $\frac{7}{8}$ kilogram. How many smaller bags were there?

8 At the end of the day, a bakery had $4\frac{1}{2}$ loaves of bread left over. There were 6 employees working for the bakery. Each employee took the same number of loaves of bread. How many loaves of bread did each employee take?

© 2020 Marshall Cavendish Education Pte Ltd

9 In a factory, $2\frac{1}{10}$ bags of flour are needed to make a batch of cookies. The factory used $8\frac{2}{5}$ bags of flour yesterday. How many batches of cookies did the factory make yesterday?

10 Natalie used $6\frac{3}{5}$ jugs of water to fill 3 similar empty tanks equally. How many jugs of water did she pour into each tank?

© 2020 Marshall Cavendish Education Pte Ltd

2 Real-World Problems: Fractions

11 Christian has a piece of ribbon that is $7\frac{4}{5}$ inches long. He cuts it into equal pieces such that each

piece is $\frac{3}{5}$ inch long. How many pieces of ribbon does he have?

12 A group of teenagers shared $15\frac{5}{6}$ pizzas. Each teenager received $\frac{5}{6}$ of a pizza. How many

teenagers were there?

© 2020 Marshall Cavendish Education Pte Ltd

Chapter 3

Extra Practice and Homework
Fractions and Decimals

Activity 3   Adding and Subtracting Decimals Fluently

Estimate. Then, add.

1
```
    1 2 . 3 3 2
  +    8 . 6 7 5
```

2
```
    6 2 . 6 9 2
  + 1 8 . 4 6
```

3
```
    1 2 . 5 7 6
  + 3 4 . 5 3 2
```

4
```
    2 9 . 9 5 9
  +    9 . 7 4 9
```

Write in vertical form. Then, add. Check if each answer is reasonable.

5 98.588 + 5.479

6 56.784 + 35.159

7 34.766 + 23.45

8 56.254 + 12.367

© 2020 Marshall Cavendish Education Pte Ltd

Estimate. Then, subtract.

9
```
   4 . 5 7 2
 − 3 . 4 3 8
───────────
```

10
```
   6 . 7 3 2
 − 4 . 3 5
───────────
```

11
```
  1 4 . 5 7 1
 −  6 . 7 9 5
────────────
```

12
```
  1 0 . 0 3 5
 −  1 . 2 4 5
────────────
```

Write in vertical form. Then, subtract. Check if each answer is reasonable.

13 34.656 − 12.92

14 67.89 − 23.498

15 12.356 − 4.376

16 34.591 − 23.87

© 2020 Marshall Cavendish Education Pte Ltd

Name: _____ Date: _____

Chapter 3 Extra Practice and Homework
Fractions and Decimals

Activity 4   Multiplying Decimals Fluently

Write in vertical form. Then, multiply.

1 0.2 × 8

2 0.17 × 7

3 0.24 × 4

4 0.524 × 10

5 0.3 × 0.3

6 0.2 × 0.5

7 0.6 × 0.6

8 0.9 × 0.8

© 2020 Marshall Cavendish Education Pte Ltd

Multiply mentally.

9 $0.6 \times 6 = $ _____

10 $0.1 \times 12 = $ _____

11 $0.3 \times 0.6 = $ _____

12 $0.4 \times 0.8 = $ _____

13 $0.15 \times 4 = $ _____

14 $0.12 \times 7 = $ _____

15 $0.023 \times 7 = $ _____

16 $0.015 \times 9 = $ _____

Rewrite decimals into fractions.

© 2020 Marshall Cavendish Education Pte Ltd

Write in vertical form. Then, multiply.

17 0.5 × 1.3

18 1.4 × 3.4

19 3.6 × 4.8

20 0.25 × 6.9

21 0.67 × 2.4

22 0.45 × 0.91

23 4.8 × 1.231

24 0.211 × 0.41

© 2020 Marshall Cavendish Education Pte Ltd

Solve.

25 Given that $2.5 \times 2.6 = 6.5$, find the value of the following.

a 2.5×0.26

b 0.25×0.26

c 7.5×2.6

d 2.5×0.52

© 2020 Marshall Cavendish Education Pte Ltd

Chapter 3

Extra Practice and Homework
Fractions and Decimals

Activity 5   Dividing Decimals Fluently

Divide.

1 8 ÷ 0.4

2 7 ÷ 0.2

3 9 ÷ 0.3

4 65 ÷ 0.5

5 32 ÷ 0.8

6 49 ÷ 0.7

© 2020 Marshall Cavendish Education Pte Ltd

7 $7 \div 0.07$

8 $8 \div 0.16$

9 $6 \div 0.08$

10 $64 \div 0.32$

11 $26 \div 0.26$

12 $81 \div 0.09$

© 2020 Marshall Cavendish Education Pte Ltd

13 $256 \div 0.4$

14 $845 \div 0.5$

15 $169 \div 0.13$

16 $0.9 \div 0.3$

17 $0.8 \div 0.4$

18 $0.7 \div 0.2$

© 2020 Marshall Cavendish Education Pte Ltd

19 $0.48 \div 0.06$

20 $0.84 \div 0.02$

21 $0.33 \div 0.3$

22 $0.63 \div 0.9$

23 $0.928 \div 0.2$

24 $0.432 \div 0.16$

© 2020 Marshall Cavendish Education Pte Ltd

25 $5.1 \div 0.3$

26 $8.55 \div 0.9$

27 $8.52 \div 1.2$

28 $25.5 \div 1.7$

29 $68.7 \div 1.5$

30 $9.03 \div 8.6$

© 2020 Marshall Cavendish Education Pte Ltd

Solve.

31 Given that 2.21 ÷ 1.3 = 1.7, find the value of the following.

a 22.1 ÷ 1.3

b 2.21 ÷ 0.13

c 2.21 ÷ 0.17

d 1.7 × 0.13

© 2020 Marshall Cavendish Education Pte Ltd

Chapter 3

Extra Practice and Homework
Fractions and Decimals

Activity 6 Real-World Problems: Decimals

Solve.

① Jose rode his bicycle for 0.75 miles and walked for 0.215 miles to reach his school. How far did he travel altogether?

② The volume of water in a tank was 9.56 liters. Nicole scooped out 0.693 liter of water from the tank. How many liters of water are left in the tank?

© 2020 Marshall Cavendish Education Pte Ltd

3 A pound of beans costs $7.80. Mr. Clark buys 6.5 pounds of beans. How much does he pay for the beans?

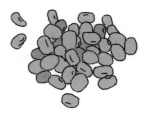

4 A store owner has 14.12 pounds of salt. He stores the salt into 8 containers equally. How many pounds of salt are there in each container?

© 2020 Marshall Cavendish Education Pte Ltd

5 The perimeter of a triangular land plot is 18.465 feet. The lengths of two of its sides are 5.6 feet and 7.54 feet. Find the length of the third side of the land plot.

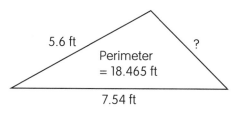

5.6 ft

Perimeter = 18.465 ft

?

7.54 ft

6 A baker uses 7.89 pounds of flour to make cookies and 2.455 pounds of flour to make muffins.

    a How many pounds of flour does the baker use in all?

    b How many more pounds of flour does the baker use for making cookies than for making muffins?

© 2020 Marshall Cavendish Education Pte Ltd

7 The height of a standing fan is 127 centimeters. 1 inch is 2.54 centimeters. What is the height of the standing fan in inches?

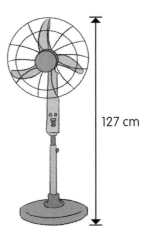

127 cm

8 Mr. Baker's car can travel 21.3 miles per gallon of petrol. The fuel tank of his car holds 13.65 gallons of petrol. How far can he travel?

© 2020 Marshall Cavendish Education Pte Ltd

9 The price of an apple is $2 and the price of a melon is $4.50. Find the total price of 5 apples and 1 melon.

Price = $2

Price = $4.50

10 Ms. Taylor buys 8 picture books and 12 markers from a book store. The price of a book is $17.85 and the price of a marker is $2.25. Calculate the total amount Ms. Taylor spends.

© 2020 Marshall Cavendish Education Pte Ltd

11 Zachary buys 9.5 pounds of flour. He uses 1.1 pounds of the flour to make bread. He keeps the rest of the flour in bags. Each small bag contains 1.2 pounds of flour. How many bags does he use?

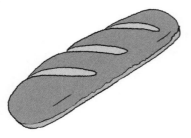

12 Mia poured 36 full bottles of water into a tank with capacity of 85.6 liters. 0.8 liter of water overflowed from the tank. Find the capacity of each bottle.

© 2020 Marshall Cavendish Education Pte Ltd

Mathematical Habit 3 Construct viable arguments

Samuel tried solving the questions involving division of fractions and division of decimals.

Samuel's solutions:

$$5 \div \frac{4}{5} = 5 \times \frac{5}{4}$$
$$= 5\frac{5}{4}$$
$$= 6\frac{1}{4}$$

$$5 \div 0.8 = \frac{5}{0.8}$$
$$= \frac{50}{8}$$
$$= \frac{25}{4}$$
$$= 6\frac{1}{4}$$
$$= 6.25$$

Chloe said that Samuel made mistakes in his solutions. Samuel did not agree with Chloe, because his answers for solving $5 \div \frac{4}{5}$ and $5 \div 0.8$ are the same. Who is correct? Explain.

© 2020 Marshall Cavendish Education Pte Ltd

1 **Mathematical Habit 1** Persevere in solving problems

Ms. Martinez bought 102 sticks of jelly. Her nephew, Devin, ate $\frac{1}{3}$ of the jelly. Her niece, Sara, ate $\frac{1}{4}$ of the remainder. Mr. Miller and Ms. Martinez ate the rest of the jelly. Mr. Miller ate twice as many sticks of jelly as her. How many sticks of jelly did Ms. Martinez eat?

2 **Mathematical Habit 1** Persevere in solving problems

A crate $\frac{1}{2}$-filled with grapes weighs 8.6 pounds. A similar crate $\frac{1}{4}$-filled with grapes weighs 3.35 pounds less than the crate $\frac{1}{2}$-filled with grapes. What is the weight of an empty crate?

© 2020 Marshall Cavendish Education Pte Ltd

Name: ______________________ Date: ______________

Chapter 4

Extra Practice and Homework

Ratio

Activity 1 Comparing Two Quantities

Write two ratios to compare the quantities.

1. 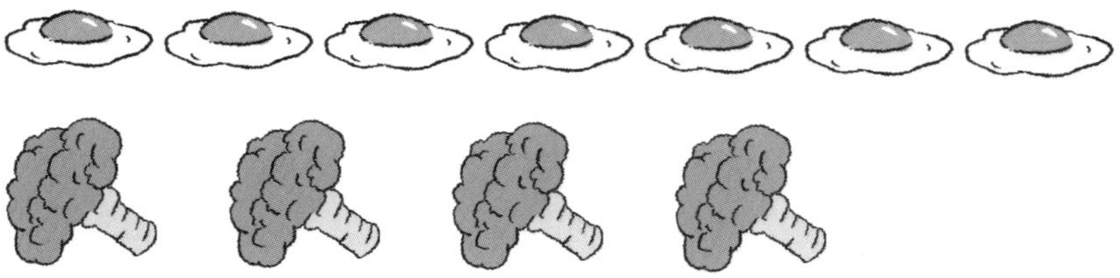

2. Kayla collects 19 cards and Tyler collects 31 cards.

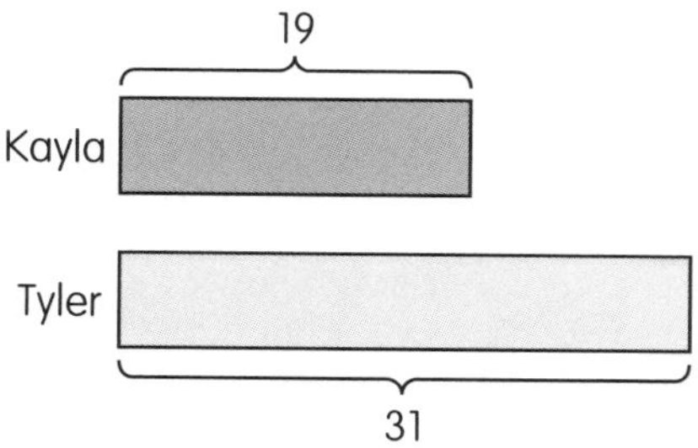

3. In a survey, 5 people said they like watching basketball and 9 people said they do not like watching basketball.

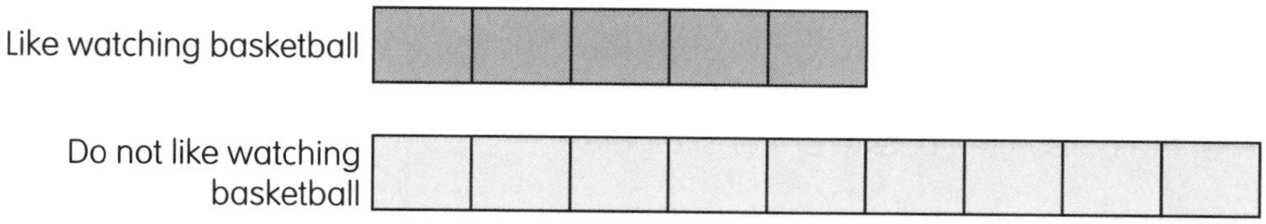

State whether each of the following can be expressed as a ratio.

4. 7 gal and 5 T

5. 36 cm and 10 m

6. 4 yd and 80 in.

7. 40 oz and 4 pt

© 2020 Marshall Cavendish Education Pte Ltd

Solve.

8 There are 94 apples in a box. 37 of them are red and the rest are green.

   a What is the ratio of the number of red apples to the number of green apples?

   b What is the ratio of the number of green apples to the total number of apples?

9 The number of meerkats is $\frac{5}{9}$ of the number of lemurs in a zoo.

   a Find the ratio of the number of meerkats to the number of lemurs.

   b Find the ratio of the number of meerkats to the total number of meerkats and lemurs.

10 There are some soccer balls and basketballs in a basket. For every 2 soccer balls, there are 5 basketballs.

   a What is the ratio of the number of soccer balls to the total number of soccer balls and basketballs in the basket?

   b What fraction of the balls in the basket are basketballs?

© 2020 Marshall Cavendish Education Pte Ltd

11 Cole had 78 tomatoes at first. After he gave away some tomatoes, he had 35 tomatoes left.

a Find the ratio of the number of tomatoes Cole had at first to the number of tomatoes he had left.

b What fraction of the number of tomatoes did Cole give away?

12 The length of a green ribbon is 8 inches and the length of a blue ribbon is 24 inches.

a How many times the length of the shorter piece is the longer piece?

b What is the ratio of the length of the longer piece to the total length of the ribbons?

13 The mass of a tin of paint is 4 kilograms and the mass of a pail of water is 6 kilograms. How many times the mass of the pail of water is the mass of the tin of paint?

© 2020 Marshall Cavendish Education Pte Ltd

14 Mr. Sanders buys 14 pounds of meat and 22 pounds of fish.

a Find the ratio of the weight of the meat to the weight of the fish.

b What fraction of the total weight of the meat and fish is the weight of the meat?

15 The ratio of the volume of blue paint to the volume of red paint is 8 : 7.

a Express the difference between the volume of blue paint and the volume of red paint as a fraction of the total volume of blue and red paint.

b Express the volume of blue paint as a fraction of twice the volume of red paint.

© 2020 Marshall Cavendish Education Pte Ltd

Chapter 4 Extra Practice and Homework
Ratio

Activity 2   Equivalent Ratios

Use division to find all whole number ratios equivalent to each of the following.

1 8 : 36

2 12 : 52

State whether each pair of ratios are equivalent.

3 12 : 27 and 4 : 9

4 4 : 7 and 24 : 42

5 9 : 6 and 6 : 9

6 12 : 52 and 4 : 13

7 8 : 36 and 4 : 18

8 63 : 14 and 18 : 4

Express each ratio in its simplest form.

9 45 : 15

10 32 : 64

11 45 : 9

12 14 : 49

13 3 yd : 3 ft

14 5 h : 52 min

15 64 oz : 6 lb

16 2 kg : 60 g

© 2020 Marshall Cavendish Education Pte Ltd

Find the missing term of each pair of equivalent ratios.

17 7 : 15 = 28 : _____

18 6 : 17 = 36 : _____

19 11 : _____ = 88 : 64

20 6 : 8 = _____ : 72

21 42 : 18 = _____ : 3

22 _____ : 24 = 7 : 6

23 48 : _____ = 3 : 5

24 65 : 90 = 13 : _____

Find the equivalent ratios.

25 Use multiplication to find three ratios equivalent to 6 : 13.

There are many possible answers. Find three of them.

26 Use division to find all the whole number ratios equivalent to 66 : 18.

Find the missing term of each pair of equivalent ratios.

27 36 : 27 = 16 : _____

28 16 : _____ = 36 : 54

29 21 : 9 = _____ : 12

30 21 : 28 = _____ : 72

31 _____ : 42 = 6 : 14

32 25 : 45 = _____ : 27

33 60 : 80 = 27 : _____

34 35 : 14 = 15 : _____

© 2020 Marshall Cavendish Education Pte Ltd

Fill in the table.

35 Diego records the amount of orange syrup and water he used to make four mixtures of orange drink using identical cups of orange syrup and water.

Mixture	A	B	C	D
Number of Cups of Orange Syrup	3	6	9	12
Number of Cups of Water	7	14	21	28
Orange Drink : Water	3 : 7			
Orange Drink : Water (Simplest form)	3 : 7			
$\dfrac{\text{Number of Cups of Orange Drink}}{\text{Numer of Cups of Water}}$	$\dfrac{3}{7}$			

What do you notice about the ratios of the four mixtures of orange drink?

Solve.

36 For every 5 gallons of dye concentrate, 12 gallons of water are added to make a dye solution.

a Find the ratio of the number of gallons of dye concentrate to the number of gallons of water needed to make the dye solution.

b How many gallons of dye concentrate are used to make 68 gallons of dye solution?

c How many gallons of dye concentrate are used when 60 gallons of water are added to make the dye solution?

© 2020 Marshall Cavendish Education Pte Ltd

37 The ratio of the cost of a book to the cost of a dictionary is 3 : 8. The ratio of the cost of a dictionary to the cost of a folder is 4 : 1. Find the ratio of the cost of the book to the cost of the dictionary to the cost of the folder.

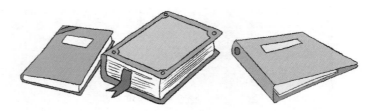

38 Sean mixes some ingredients to make regular cups of smoothie. The ratio of the amount of yogurt to the amount of blueberry juice to the amount of milk used is the same for all cups. The table shows the different amounts of ingredients used in making regular cups of smoothie. Find the missing numbers in the table.

Number of Regular Cups	Amount of Ingredients (ml)		
	Yogurt	Blueberry Juice	Milk
1			240
2	60	160	
3		240	720

© 2020 Marshall Cavendish Education Pte Ltd

Chapter

4

Extra Practice and Homework
Ratio

Activity 3   Real-World Problems: Ratios

Solve.

1 The cost of a carpet is $45. Daniel and Sophia bought the carpet and share the cost in the ratio 4 : 5. How much did Daniel pay for the carpet?

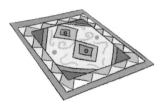

2 A group of students surveyed chose badminton and soccer as their favorite sport in the ratio 4 : 7.

   a If 63 students chose soccer as their favorite sport, find the number of students that chose badminton as their favorite sport.

   b If 132 students were surveyed, find the number of students that chose soccer as their favorite sport.

© 2020 Marshall Cavendish Education Pte Ltd

3 Some stickers were divided among Ava, Brianna and Carson in the ratio 1 : 3 : 4. Brianna received 21 stickers.

    a How many stickers did Ava receive?

    b How many stickers were there in all?

4 Mariah bought a packet of mixed nuts. The ratio of the weight of almonds to the weight of walnuts to the weight of pecans in ounces is 4 : 3 : 8. The weight of pecans is 80 ounces.

    a Find the weight of the walnuts.

    a Find the total weight of the packet of mixed nuts.

© 2020 Marshall Cavendish Education Pte Ltd

5 David has a box of red, blue, and green pens. The ratio of the number of red pens to the number of blue pens is 5 : 2. The ratio of the number of blue pens to the number of green pens is 3 : 5. What is the ratio of the number of red pens to the number of green pens?

 6 Layla, Sofia, and Evelyn share a box of 754 pieces of colored paper. The ratio of Layla's pieces of colored paper to Sofia's pieces of colored paper is 4 : 3. The ratio of Sofia's pieces of colored paper to Evelyn's pieces of colored paper is 9 : 5.

a How many piece of colored paper does Layla have?

b How many more pieces of colored paper does Layla have than Evelyn?

© 2020 Marshall Cavendish Education Pte Ltd

7 At a party, the ratio of the number of adults to the number of children was 5 : 3. Halfway through the party, 20 adults left and the ratio became 5 : 4. How many children were there at the party?

8 The ratio of the amount of money Rachel saved to the amount of money Timothy saved was 12 : 13. After Timothy spent $27, Rachel had 3 times as much as Timothy.

a How much did Rachel save?

b How much did they save altogether at first?

© 2020 Marshall Cavendish Education Pte Ltd

9 Kyle and Claire bought a present and shared the cost in the ratio 3 : 8. Claire paid $15 more than Kyle. Find the total cost of the present.

10 Evan, Luke, and Aidan sold magnets in the ratio 5 : 3 : 4 to raise funds for their Scout troop. Luke sold 81 magnets. How many magnets did Evan and Aidan sell in all?

© 2020 Marshall Cavendish Education Pte Ltd

11 The ratio of Grace's savings to Ryan's savings is 3 : 5, and the ratio of Ryan's savings to Julia's savings is 11 : 4. The difference between Grace's and Julia's savings is $65. Calculate the amount of Julia's savings.

12 A 54-inch long ribbon is cut into 3 strips in the ratio 2 : 3 : 5.

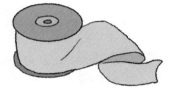

a What is the length of the longest piece?

b How much longer is the longest piece than the shortest piece?

c What is the length of the shortest piece if they were cut in the ratio 1 : 2 : 3?

© 2020 Marshall Cavendish Education Pte Ltd

13. The ratio of the number of cheese muffins to the number of chocolate muffins in a confectionery was 3 : 2. After 144 cheese muffins were sold, the ratio of the number of cheese muffins to the number of chocolate muffins changed to 3 : 5. How many more cheese muffins than chocolate muffins were there at first?

14. Adam, Bryan and Juan had a total of 48 apples. They shared the apples in the ratio 5 : 7 : 12.

a How many fewer apples did Bryan have than Juan?

b If the boys decided to share the apples in the ratio 3 : 4 : 5 instead, how many more apples would Bryan have than Adam?

© 2020 Marshall Cavendish Education Pte Ltd

15 The ratio of the number of students who walk to school to the total number of students in a school is 2 : 5.

a What is the ratio of the number of students who walk to school to those who do not?

b There are 168 students who do not walk to school. How many students walk to the school?

c 8 students who do not walk to school now walk to school. What is the new ratio of the number of students who walk to school to those who do not?

© 2020 Marshall Cavendish Education Pte Ltd

1 | Mathematical Habit **6** | Use precise mathematical language

Describe a situation that the ratio 7 : 8 could represent.

2 | Mathematical Habit **3** | Construct viable arguments

Hannah is 12 years old and her sister, Olivia, is 10 years old. Hannah says the ratio of her age to Olivia's age is 6 : 5. Olivia says the ratio of Hannah's age to her age is still 6 : 5 after 4 years. Explain why Olivia is incorrect.

© 2020 Marshall Cavendish Education Pte Ltd

1 | Mathematical Habit 1 | **Perservere in solving problems**

Mr. King buys some ham slices, wheat wraps, and cheese for $90. The ratio of the amount of money he spends on cheese to the amount he spends on ham is 2 : 3. The ratio of the amount of money he spends on cheese to the amount he spends on wheat wraps is 6 : 5. The cost of each ham slice is $0.75.

a How much does Mr. King spend on the ham slices?

b How many ham slices does Mr. King buy?

2 | Mathematical Habit 1 | **Perservere in solving problems**

In a bakery, the ratio of the number of apple pies to the number of croissants was 5 : 3. After 6 apple pies were sold and 6 more croissants were made, the ratio became 7 : 5. How many apple pies and how many croissants were there in the bakery at first?

© 2020 Marshall Cavendish Education Pte Ltd

Chapter

Extra Practice and Homework
Rates and Speed

Activity 1   Rates and Unit Rates

Solve.

1. It takes 9 minutes for a flowing faucet to fill up a 27-gallon tank. How much water flows from the faucet in 1 minute?

 2. A printing machine can print 735 books in 5 minutes. How many books are printed per minute?

© 2020 Marshall Cavendish Education Pte Ltd

3 A truck needs 6 gallons of gas to travel 186 miles. What is the rate of the distance traveled by the truck in miles per gallon of gas?

4 Ms. Hughes pays $2,191 to stay one week in a hotel. How much does she pay per day?

© 2020 Marshall Cavendish Education Pte Ltd

5 It took Ms. Hill 6 hours to paint a wall surface with an area of 282 square feet. How many square feet did Ms. Hill paint in 1 hour?

6 A fax machine can transmit 6 pages in 1 minute. How many pages can the fax machine transmit in 7 minutes?

© 2020 Marshall Cavendish Education Pte Ltd

7 A wheel makes 35 revolutions per minute. How many minutes does the wheel take to make 315 revolutions?

8 Ms. Walker earns $12.50 per hour working at a book store. Fill in the table.

Number of Hours	Amount Earned
1	$12.50
2	
3	
4	
5	

© 2020 Marshall Cavendish Education Pte Ltd

9 The table shows the cost of three different types of rice sold at a grocery store. Fill in the table. Round your answers to the nearest hundredth of a dollar.

Type of Rice	Amount Paid	Amount Purchased	Cost per Pound
Polished	$20.60	10 lb	
Brown	$9.60	3 lb	
Wild		2 lb	$4.20

Which type of rice costs the most per pound?

© 2020 Marshall Cavendish Education Pte Ltd

10 Shop A sells chocolates at $24.20 for a 14-ounce box and Shop B sells the same chocolates at $19.90 for a 12-ounce box. Which shop has a better deal? Explain how you arrived at your answer. Round your answers to 2 decimal places.

© 2020 Marshall Cavendish Education Pte Ltd

Chapter

5

Extra Practice and Homework
Rates and Speed

Activity 2   Real-World Problems: Rates and Unit Rates

Solve.

1 A printing machine can print 335 copies in 5 minutes. At this rate, how many copies can the machine print in an hour?

2 Water flowing from a faucet can fill $\frac{1}{4}$ of a tank in 5 minutes.

   a How long does it take to fill the tank completely with water?

   b How long does it take to fill 7 similar tanks completely with water? Give your answer in hours and minutes.

© 2020 Marshall Cavendish Education Pte Ltd

3 The table below shows the parking fees for a park.

From 9:00 A.M. to 5:00 P.M.	$5.50 per hour
After 5:00 P.M.	$7.00 per hour

Ms. Jones parked at the park from 4:00 P.M. to 9:00 P.M. How much did she pay for the parking fees?

4 A van travels 125 miles on 5 gallons of gasoline.

a Find the distance the van can travel if the fuel tank contains 12 gallons of gasoline.

b Find the amount of gasoline the van uses to travel 180 miles.

© 2020 Marshall Cavendish Education Pte Ltd

5 Ms. Scott earns $14.50 per hour working at a bakery. Fill in the table.

Number of Hours	Amount Earned
1	$14.50
2	
3	
4	
5	

a How much will Ms. Scott earn if she works 3 hours?

b How many hours will Ms. Scott have to work to earn $58?

6 The table shows the cost of three different types of flour sold at a grocery store. Fill in the table. Round your answers to the nearest hundredth of a dollar.

Type of Flour	Amount Paid	Amount Purchased	Cost per Pound
Cake	$21.60	10 lb	
Pastry	$8.60	2 lb	
Self-raising		4 lb	$5.20

a Which type of flour costs the most per pound?

b What is the price difference per pound between the most expensive flour and the cheapest flour?

© 2020 Marshall Cavendish Education Pte Ltd

7 The table shows the charges for renting a room for functions.

First Four Hours	$1,800
Every Additional Hour	$500

Mr. Cooper rents the room for 9 hours. How much does he pay in total?

8 The table below shows the rates for renting cars from WIN car rental company.

First Day (Monday to Friday)	$75
Every Additional Day (Monday to Friday)	$60
Weekend (Saturday and Sunday)	$80

a How much does it cost to rent a car for 3 weekdays?

b How much does it cost to rent a car on Wednesday, and keep it for an entire week?

c The rate for renting cars from BEST car rental company is a flat rate of $70 per day. If Ms. Phillips wants to rent a car for one week, starting on Wednesday, which car rental company would be better? Explain your answer.

© 2020 Marshall Cavendish Education Pte Ltd

9 A machine dyes an equal number of same-sized shirts every hour. The line graph shows the number of shirts dyed by the machine over 6 hours.

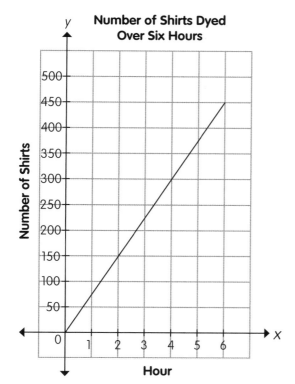

a How many shirts does the machine dye per hour?

b How long does the machine take to dye 375 shirts?

© 2020 Marshall Cavendish Education Pte Ltd

10 A book store rents comic books. The line graph shows the cost of rental for comic books by the book store.

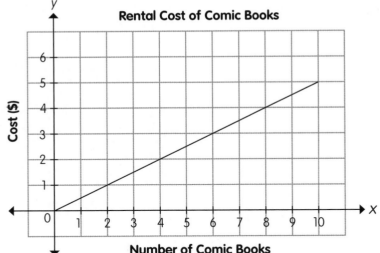

Rental Cost of Comic Books

a What is the total rental cost for 5 comic books?

b William borrowed 12 comic books. How much does he pay for the rental in total?

© 2020 Marshall Cavendish Education Pte Ltd

Chapter 5

Extra Practice and Homework
Rates and Speed

Activity 3   Distance and Speed

Solve.

1. A car travels at a speed of 55 miles per hour. How far will it travel in 5 hours?

2. A school bus travels at a speed of 48 kilometers per hour. How long will it take to travel 120 kilometers?

© 2020 Marshall Cavendish Education Pte Ltd

3 A train travels at a speed of 86 miles per hour. How many miles will the train travel in $2\frac{1}{2}$ hours?

4 A mouse runs a distance of 3 meters in 20 seconds. What is its speed in meters per second?

© 2020 Marshall Cavendish Education Pte Ltd

5   A bee flew at a speed of 9 inches per second. It travels a distance of 81 inches. How long did the bee fly?

6   Mr. Reed cycles for 72 kilometers in 1.5 hours. He continues to cycle at this rate. How many kilometers will he travel in 3.5 hours?

© 2020 Marshall Cavendish Education Pte Ltd

7 An airplane traveled 5,138 kilometers from Country A to Country B in 7 hours, and traveled 6,013 kilometers from Country B to Country C in the same amount of time.

a What was the speed of the airplane when it traveled from Country A to Country B?

b What was the speed of the airplane when it traveled from Country B to Country C?

© 2020 Marshall Cavendish Education Pte Ltd

Chapter

5

Extra Practice and Homework
Rates and Speed

Activity 4 Average Speed

Solve.

1. Julian walked from his house for 2 hours at a speed of 4 miles per hour to the library. He then returned home by bicycle at a speed of 12 miles per hour. Find his average speed for the whole journey in miles per hour.

> Find the total distance traveled and the time taken to calculate average speed.

2. Leah drove for 2 hours at a speed of 60 miles per hour, and for 3 hours at 50 miles per hour. What was her average speed in miles per hour for the whole journey?

© 2020 Marshall Cavendish Education Pte Ltd

3 Austin walked 3 kilometers from his house to Park A. He then walked another 4 kilometers from Park A to Park B. The total time he took to walk was 84 minutes. Find Austin's average speed in kilometers per hour.

4 Brooke cycled at an average speed of 22 kilometers per hour from her house to the nearby park, and cycled back at an average speed of 14 kilometers per hour via the same route. She took 66 minutes to cycle back to her house. How long, in minutes, did she take to cycle from her house to the nearby park?

© 2020 Marshall Cavendish Education Pte Ltd

Chapter

5

Extra Practice and Homework
Rates and Speed

Activity 5   Real-World Problems: Speed and Average Speed

Solve.

1 Ms. Lee takes 5 hours to drive 210 miles from her house to the Central Park. Her average speed for the first 2 hours is 50 miles per hour. Find her average speed for the last 3 hours.

2 Ms. Morris drives her car for 1 hour 30 minutes with a constant speed of 70 kilometers per hour. She then drives for another 45 minutes at a constant speed of 80 kilometers per hour. How far does she drive?

© 2020 Marshall Cavendish Education Pte Ltd

3 A train moved at a speed of 90 miles per hour for 2 hours, and then slowed down to 72 miles per hour for the next 30 minutes.

    a Find the total distance the train traveled.

    b Find the average speed of the train.

4 Connor and Riley left a cafeteria at the same time and cycled in opposite directions. Both of them cycled at constant speeds. Connor cycled at a speed of 140 meters per minute. At the end of 30 minutes, they were 7,800 meters apart. Find Riley's cycling speed in meters per minute.

© 2020 Marshall Cavendish Education Pte Ltd

5 Mr. Evans and Mr. Lopez stay at the same place. Mr. Evans drives 64.8 kilometers from work to home at a speed of 48 kilometers per hour. Mr. Lopez drives 130 kilometers from work to home at a speed of 65 kilometers per hour. They both leave their work places at the same time.

a Who arrives home first?

b What is the difference in time for them to reach home?

© 2020 Marshall Cavendish Education Pte Ltd

6 Ms. Chavez had a dinner appointment at her friend's house at 5:30 P.M. She left her house at 11:00 A.M. and traveled in her car at an average speed of 56 miles per hour to her friend's house that was 350 miles away. What time did Ms. Chavez reach her friend's house? Was she late for the dinner appointment?

© 2020 Marshall Cavendish Education Pte Ltd

Mathematical Habit 4 Use mathematical models

A plumber pays $3.60 for 60 centimeters of pipe. Explain how the plumber can use the unit cost of the pipe to find the cost of buying 100 meters of the same kind of pipe. Show the calculations the plumber needs to make.

MATH JOURNAL

© 2020 Marshall Cavendish Education Pte Ltd

Mathematical Habit 1 Persevere in solving problems

A car started traveling at 9:00 A.M. from City A to City B with a constant speed of 70 kilometers per hour. A truck started traveling at the same time as the car from City B to City A with a constant speed of 50 kilometers per hour. The car and the truck passed each other at 4:00 P.M.

a What is the distance from City A to City B?

b What time did the car reach City B?

c How far away was the truck from City A when the car reached City B?

© 2020 Marshall Cavendish Education Pte Ltd

Chapter 6 Extra Practice and Homework
Percent

Activity 1 Understanding Percent

Solve.

1. Out of a total of 400 students in a school, 245 of them wear glasses. What percent of the students in the school wear glasses?

2. Of the 500 vehicles that passed a junction, 108 are taxis. What percent of the vehicles that passed the junction are taxis?

3. Of the 300 plants in a park, 180 are trees and the rest are flowering bushes. What percent of the plants in the park are trees?

4. Out of 40 questions, Jordan answered 18 of them incorrectly. What percent of the questions did he answer correctly?

© 2020 Marshall Cavendish Education Pte Ltd

Express each percent as a fraction or a mixed number in simplest form.

5 64%

6 86%

7 129%

8 160%

9 215%

10 375%

11 675%

12 789%

Rewrite each percent as a fraction with denominator of 100. Then, simplify the fraction.

© 2020 Marshall Cavendish Education Pte Ltd

Express each percent as a decimal.

13 7%

14 46%

15 75%

16 99%

17 123%

18 367%

19 475%

20 580%

Rewrite each percent as a fraction with denominator of 100 first. Then, write the fraction as a decimal.

© 2020 Marshall Cavendish Education Pte Ltd

Solve.

21 In a bakery, 14 chocolate tarts, 24 strawberry tarts, and 10 cheese tarts are made. What percent of the tarts are chocolate?

22 The table shows the number of books loaned out at a library in one week.

Monday	Tuesday	Wednesday	Thursday	Friday
12	42	30	56	10

What percent of the total number of books were loaned out on Wednesday?

© 2020 Marshall Cavendish Education Pte Ltd

Chapter

Extra Practice and Homework
Percent

Activity 2   Fractions, Decimals, and Percents

Express each fraction or mixed number as a percent.

1 $\frac{3}{5}$

2 $\frac{7}{8}$

3 $\frac{9}{15}$

4 $\frac{11}{20}$

5 $\frac{13}{25}$

6 $5\frac{3}{10}$

7 $3\frac{3}{4}$

8 $8\frac{17}{20}$

© 2020 Marshall Cavendish Education Pte Ltd

Express each decimal as a percent.

9 0.07

10 0.78

11 0.6

12 4.05

13 6.25

14 32.5

Express each percent as a fraction in simplest form.

15 0.8%

16 13.25%

© 2020 Marshall Cavendish Education Pte Ltd

17 45.5%

18 $33\frac{1}{3}$%

19 $57\frac{2}{5}$%

20 $87\frac{1}{2}$%

Express each fraction as a percent. Round your answer to the nearest whole number.

21 $\frac{96}{200}$

22 $\frac{84}{125}$

23 $\frac{96}{216}$

24 $\frac{145}{450}$

© 2020 Marshall Cavendish Education Pte Ltd

Find the missing fractions and decimals.

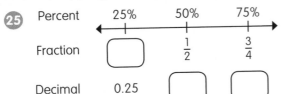 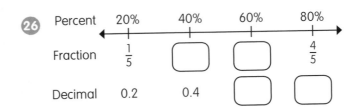

25

Percent	25%	50%	75%
Fraction	⬜	$\frac{1}{2}$	$\frac{3}{4}$
Decimal	0.25	⬜	⬜

26

Percent	20%	40%	60%	80%
Fraction	$\frac{1}{5}$	⬜	⬜	$\frac{4}{5}$
Decimal	0.2	0.4	⬜	⬜

Solve.

27 A group of children were surveyed and asked to name their favorite color. The table shows the results of the survey.

Red	Orange	Green	Blue	Yellow
16	20	40	14	30

a What percent of the students prefered green?

b What percent of the students prefered the least favorite color?

c What percent of the students prefered yellow or orange?

© 2020 Marshall Cavendish Education Pte Ltd

Chapter 6

Extra Practice and Homework
Percent

Activity 3   Percent of a Quantity

Solve. Use the bar model to help you.

1   What is 25% of 82 hours?

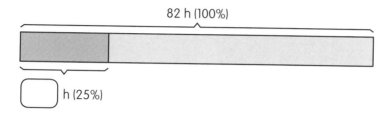

2   Luis ran 68 meters and Mandy ran 55% of the distance Luis ran. How far did Mandy run?

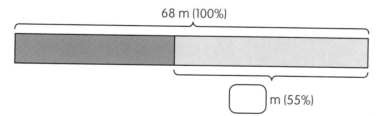

Find the quantity represented by each percent.

3   36% of 540 gallons

4   110% of $610

© 2020 Marshall Cavendish Education Pte Ltd

Solve.

5 15% of a number is 30. Find the number.

6 45% of a number is 180. Find the number.

7 175% of a number is 91. Find the number.

8 350% of a number is 2,205. Find the number.

© 2020 Marshall Cavendish Education Pte Ltd

9 A bean bag is filled with red and green beans. Of the total number of beans, 30% are red. There are 720 red beans. How many beans are there in the bag?

10 Lillian makes 480 sandwiches. 25% of them are tuna sandwiches, 45% of them are ham sandwiches, and the rest are egg sandwiches. How many egg sandwiches does Lillian make?

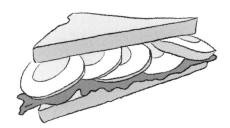

© 2020 Marshall Cavendish Education Pte Ltd

11 Ms. Stewart has $660. She uses 30% of her money to buy a dress and 20% of the remainder to buy a pair of shoes. How much does she have left?

12 42% of the pages in a book have pictures and the rest have no pictures. There are 462 pages with pictures in the book.

a What is the total number of pages in the book?

b How many pages in the book have no pictures?

© 2020 Marshall Cavendish Education Pte Ltd

13 Alyssa, James, and Ella plant seedlings in their school garden. Alyssa plants 40% of the total number of seedlings, James plants 35% of the total number of seedlings, and Ella plants the rest of the seedlings. Ella plants 88 seedlings. How many seedlings do the three children plant altogether?

14 A box contains 160 pieces of fruit. 15% of the pieces of fruit are apples, 25% of the remaining are melons, and the rest are oranges. How many oranges are there in the box?

© 2020 Marshall Cavendish Education Pte Ltd

15 At a school carnival, 95% are students and the rest are teachers. There are 800 people at the carnival.

a How many students are there at the school carnival?

b 45% of the students at the school carnival wear watches. How many students do not wear watches?

c How many teachers are there at the school carnival?

d 40% of the teachers wear watches. How many teachers do not wear watches?

© 2020 Marshall Cavendish Education Pte Ltd

© 2020 Marshall Cavendish Education Pte Ltd

Chapter 6
Extra Practice and Homework
Percent

Activity 4   Real-World Problems: Percent

Solve. Check that each answer is reasonable.

1 Destiny collects 90 bottles to recycle. 27 of the bottles are plastic and the rest are glass.

   a What percent of the bottles are plastic?

   b What percent of the bottles are glass?

2 A salesperson receives a 5% commission on the sale of each house. The commission for a house is $690. What is the price of the house?

3) Ms. Cox and her three friends are dining at a restaurant. The food they order costs $80. The bill includes an additional 15% service charge. How much does each person pay if they share the bill equally?

4) Mr. Brooks has a budget of $2,000 to buy a washing machine. The price of the washing machine he wants to buy is $1,450. Does Mr. Brooks have enough money to purchase the washing machine given that the sales tax is 10%? Explain your answer.

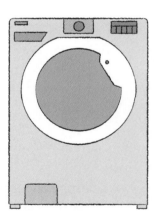

© 2020 Marshall Cavendish Education Pte Ltd

5 Mr. Ward invests $45,000 in a bank at the beginning of the year. He will receive an interest rate of 8% per year, but he will have to pay a 15% tax on the interest received.

a How much interest will Mr. Ward earn at the end of a year, after paying the tax?

b What percent of Mr. Ward's investment is the interest after paying the tax?

c How much interest will Mr. Ward earn at the end of $\frac{1}{2}$ year, after paying the tax?

© 2020 Marshall Cavendish Education Pte Ltd

6. Mr. Collins buys a table and sofa for $2,028. The table costs 30% of the price of the sofa. What is the price of the sofa?

7. There are 1,800 pastries in a bakery shop. 45% of them are pretzels and the rest are croissants. 30% of the pretzels are coated with chocolate. 70% of the croissants are coated with chocolate.

   a How many croissants are there in the bakery shop?

   b How many pretzels are coated with chocolate?

   c How many croissants are coated with chocolate?

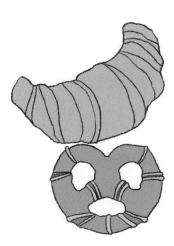

© 2020 Marshall Cavendish Education Pte Ltd

Mathematical Habit 3 Construct viable arguments

Joshua answered the following question incorrectly.

In the figure, the area of the shaded part, *DGHI*, is 37.5% of the area of rectangle *ADFE*. Rectangle *ADFE* is 80% of the area of rectangle *ABCD*. What percent of rectangle *ABCD* is shaded?

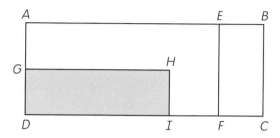

Joshua's solution:

Percent of rectangle *ABCD* that is shaded $= \dfrac{37.5}{80} \times 100\%$

$= 46.875\%$

46.875% of rectangle *ABCD* is shaded.

Explain Joshua's mistake.

© 2020 Marshall Cavendish Education Pte Ltd

Mathematical Habit 1 Persevere in solving problems

20% of the books in a library are fiction, and the rest are non-fiction. When 30% of the fiction books and 15% of the non-fiction books are borrowed, there are 1,312 books left in the library. How many books are borrowed?

© 2020 Marshall Cavendish Education Pte Ltd